Baby's FIRST YEAR

CONTENTS

DK

DORLING KINDERSLEY

London • New York • Stuttgart

D1736538

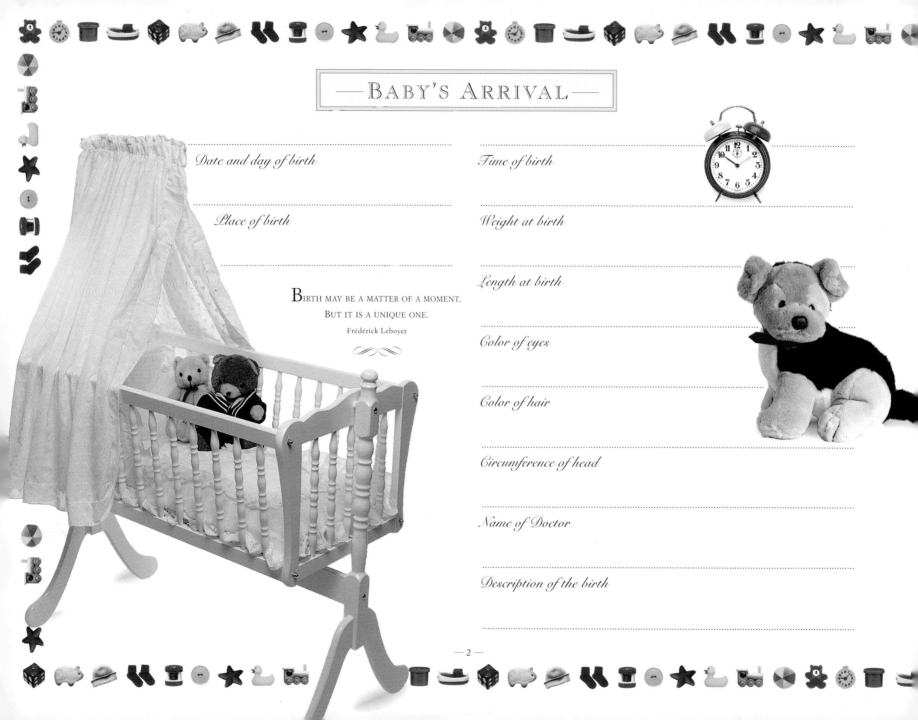

— Baby's Arrival —

Date and day of birth

Place of birth

> Birth may be a matter of a moment.
> But it is a unique one.
>
> Frédérick Leboyer

Time of birth

Weight at birth

Length at birth

Color of eyes

Color of hair

Circumference of head

Name of Doctor

Description of the birth

Baby's Photograph

Baby's appearance

....

Birth cards received

Monday's child is fair of face,
Tuesday's child is full of grace,
Wednesday's child is full of woe,
Thursday's child has far to go,
Friday's child is loving and giving,
Saturday's child works hard for a living,
And the child that is born on the Sabbath day
Is bonny and blithe, and good and gay.

Horoscope

Zodiac sign

Chinese horoscope

Birthstone

Flower

BIRTH ANNOUNCEMENT

FIRST DAYS

First visitors

Their comments

Feeding schedule

Baby's feeding times

Duration of a feeding

Description of a feeding

Sleeping schedule

Sleeping times

Wakeful times

Favorite sleeping position

Mother's feelings

Father's feelings

A BABE IS FED WITH MILK AND PRAISE.

Charles and Mary Lamb

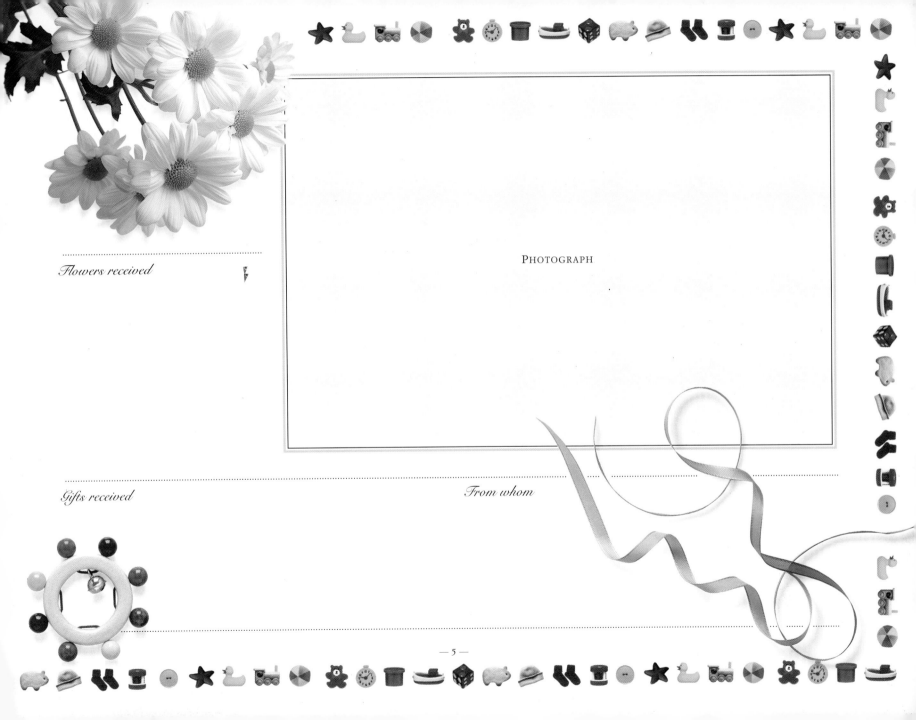

Flowers received

PHOTOGRAPH

Gifts received

From whom

Baptism

INVITATION

Description of ceremony

Guests attending

Gifts received

Your baby's behavior

Your baby's outfit

Godparents

GIVING A NAME IS INDEED A POETIC ART.
Thomas Carlyle

FAMILY TREE

Maternal

Paternal

Great–Grandmother
....
....

Great–Grandfather
....

Great–Grandmother
....
....

Great–Grandfather
....

Great–Grandmother
....
....

Great–Grandfather
....

Great–Grandmother
....
....

Great–Grandfather
....

Grandmother
....
....

Grandfather
....
....

Grandmother
....
....

Grandfather
....
....

Mother
....

Father
....

Sisters
....

Baby
....

Brothers
....

─ FIRST FOODS ─

Most babies are introduced to solid foods at between three and six months old, and will relish discovering new tastes and textures.

Little Miss Muffet sat on a tuffet
Eating her curds and whey.
Along came a spider, and sat down beside her
And frightened Miss Muffet away.

Date your baby first:

Ate puréed food

Ate solid food

Ate with a spoon

Ate in a high chair

Drank from a cup

The Queen of Hearts, she made some tarts,
All on a summer day;
The Knave of Hearts, he stole those tarts,
And took them quite away!

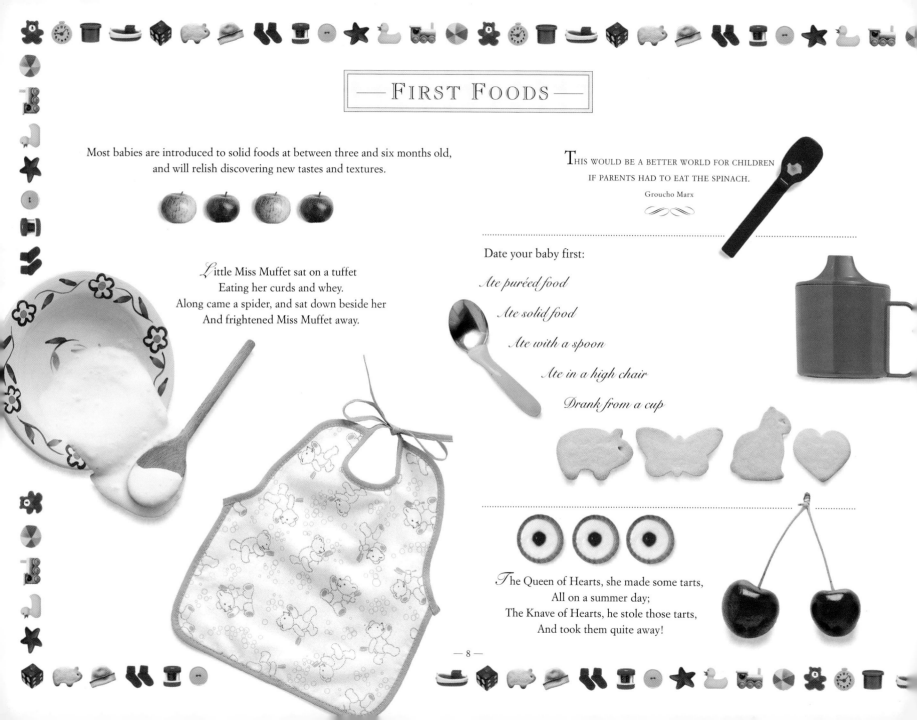

Favorite food

Description of a meal

Date of weaning

TEETHING

ADAM AND EVE HAD MANY ADVANTAGES, BUT THE PRINCIPAL ONE WAS THAT THEY ESCAPED TEETHING.

Mark Twain

A baby cuts 20 primary or milk teeth, which begin to be replaced with permanent teeth when the child is about six years old. The appearance of the first tooth is a milestone in a baby's life, although it can cause a great deal of discomfort. Some babies find chewing on a teething ring soothes the gums and helps lessen the pain.

Date of first tooth

Date of second tooth

Date of third tooth

Date of fourth tooth

Date of fifth tooth

Teething symptoms

Notes

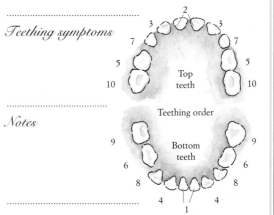

Top teeth

Teething order

Bottom teeth

NIGHT TIME

PEOPLE WHO SAY THEY SLEEP LIKE A BABY USUALLY DON'T HAVE ONE.

Leo J. Burke

Bedtime ....

Favorite sleeping position ....

Wakes at ....

Bedtime comforters ....

First sleeps through night ....

First sleeps in crib ....

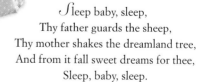

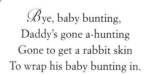

*B*ye, baby bunting,
Daddy's gone a-hunting
Gone to get a rabbit skin
To wrap his baby bunting in.

*S*leep baby, sleep,
Thy father guards the sheep,
Thy mother shakes the dreamland tree,
And from it fall sweet dreams for thee,
Sleep, baby, sleep.

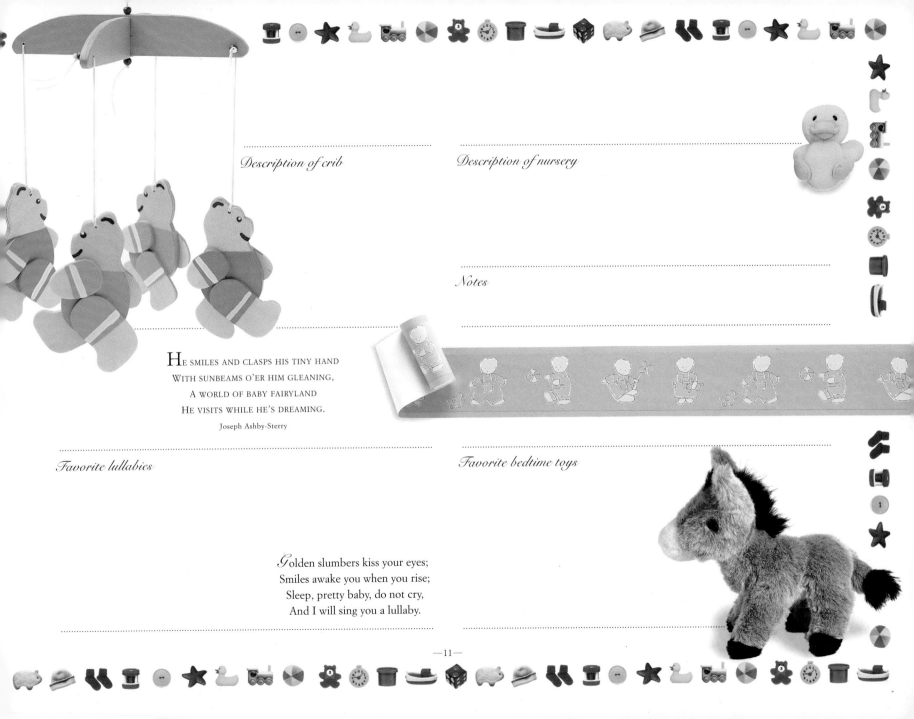

Description of crib

Description of nursery

Notes

HE SMILES AND CLASPS HIS TINY HAND
WITH SUNBEAMS O'ER HIM GLEANING,
A WORLD OF BABY FAIRYLAND
HE VISITS WHILE HE'S DREAMING.

Joseph Ashby-Sterry

Favorite lullabies

Favorite bedtime toys

Golden slumbers kiss your eyes;
Smiles awake you when you rise;
Sleep, pretty baby, do not cry,
And I will sing you a lullaby.

FAVORITE THINGS

Your baby's favorite:

....

Mobile

THE CHILDHOOD SHOWS THE MAN, AS MORNING
SHOWS THE DAY.

John Milton

Toys

....

Pictures

....

Books

Cuddly toys

....

Objects

Games

Activities

Sounds

Words

People

Animals

Stories

Songs and Nursery Rhymes

*H*ey diddle diddle
The cat and the fiddle,
The cow jumped over the moon;
The little dog laughed
To see such sport,
And the dish ran away with the spoon.

—Bathtime and Water Play—

First enjoys bath

....

First time in a big bathtub

....

Response to being bathed

....

Response to hair being washed

....

Favorite bath toys

....

Bathtime activities

....

*R*ow, row, row your boat
Gently down the stream
Merrily, merrily, merrily, merrily,
Life is but a dream.

*O*ne, two, three, four, five,
Once I caught a fish alive,
Six, seven, eight, nine, ten,
Then I let him go again.
Why did you let him go?
Because he bit my finger so.
Which finger did he bite?
This little finger on the right.

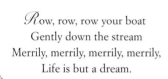

First water play in garden

First play in wading pool

First swim in swimming pool

Your baby's swimwear

PHOTOGRAPH

Favorite water games

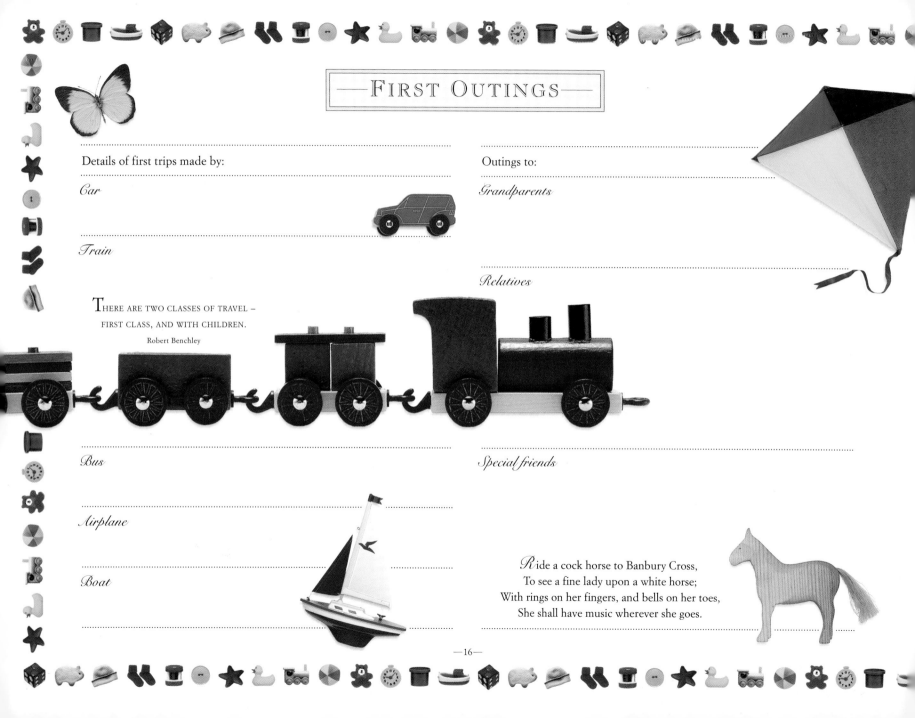

FIRST OUTINGS

Details of first trips made by:

Car

Train

> THERE ARE TWO CLASSES OF TRAVEL –
> FIRST CLASS, AND WITH CHILDREN.
>
> Robert Benchley

Bus

Airplane

Boat

Outings to:

Grandparents

Relatives

Special friends

> *R*ide a cock horse to Banbury Cross,
> To see a fine lady upon a white horse;
> With rings on her fingers, and bells on her toes,
> She shall have music wherever she goes.

Outings to:

Parks and playgrounds

Beaches

The countryside

Stores

To market, to market,
To buy a fat pig,
Home again, home again,
Jiggetty jig.

Notes

PHOTOGRAPH

First Christmas

At Christmas play and make good cheer,
For Christmas comes but once a year.

Thomas Tusser

Christmas Day:

Where it was spent

....

Who it was spent with

....

Your present to your baby

....

Stocking gifts

....

Gifts received   *From whom*

....

Description of the holidays

....

Christmas Eve

Where it was spent

....

Who it was spent with

....

Description of Christmas Eve

....

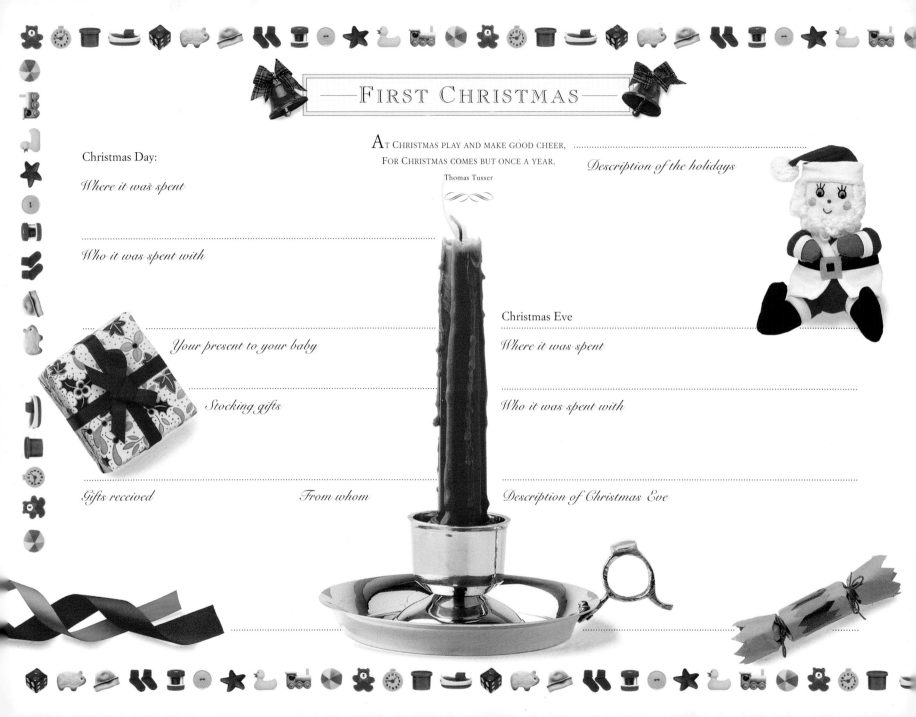

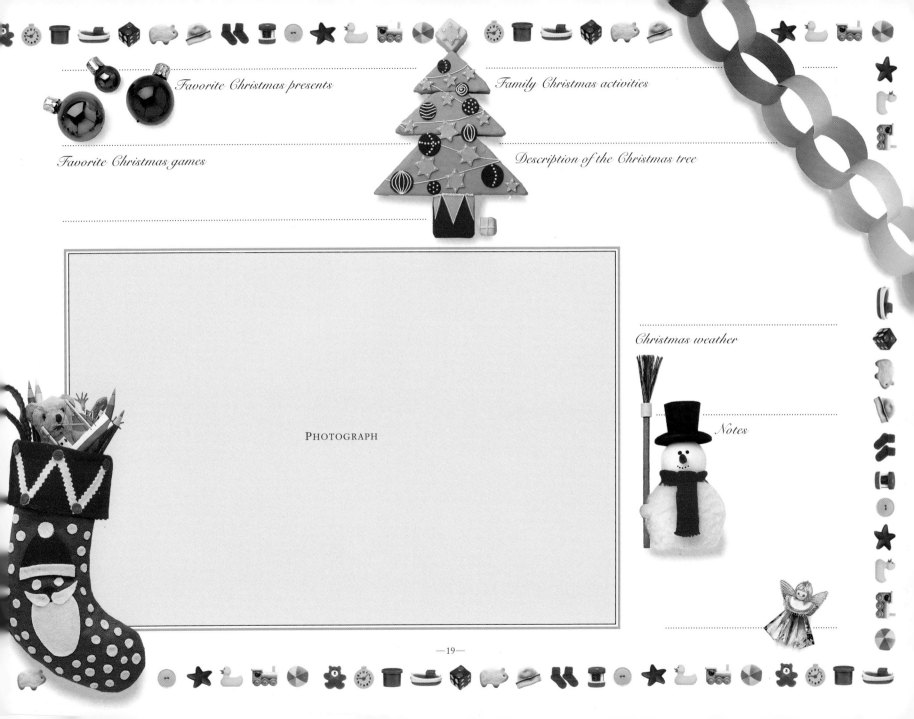

Favorite Christmas presents

Family Christmas activities

Favorite Christmas games

Description of the Christmas tree

PHOTOGRAPH

Christmas weather

Notes

—First Vacation—

Date

Place

Who was there

Travel details

Accommodation

Favorite activities

Favorite outings

Baby's behavior

Baby's new friends

PHOTOGRAPH

Notes

It is a happy talent to know how to play.

Ralph Waldo Emerson

Favorite memories of the vacation

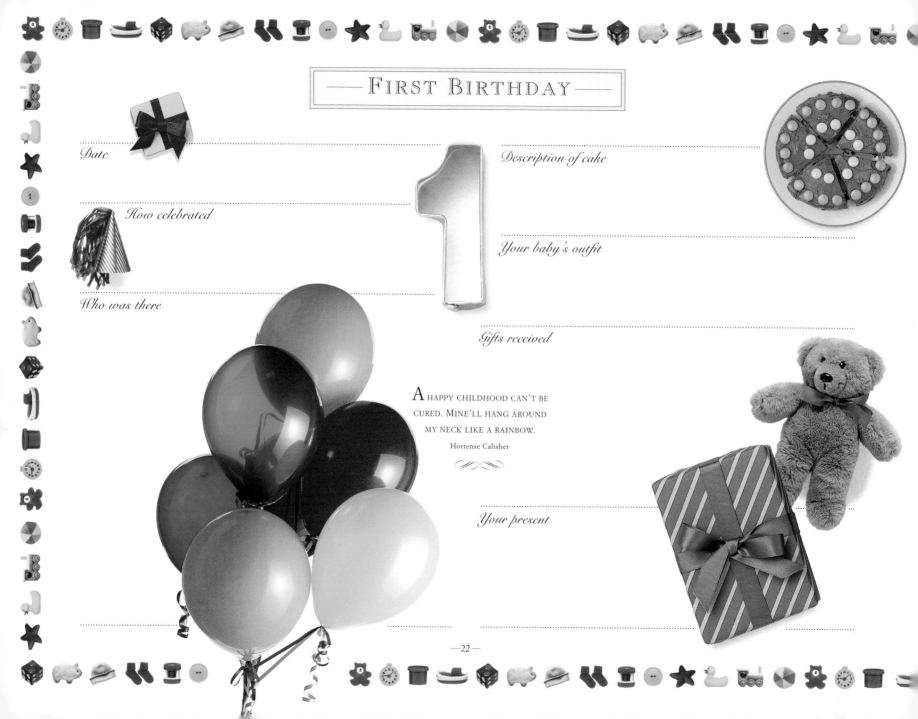

FIRST BIRTHDAY

Date ....

How celebrated ....

Who was there ....

Description of cake ....

Your baby's outfit ....

Gifts received ....

A HAPPY CHILDHOOD CAN'T BE
CURED. MINE'LL HANG AROUND
MY NECK LIKE A RAINBOW.

Hortense Calisher

Your present ....

—22—

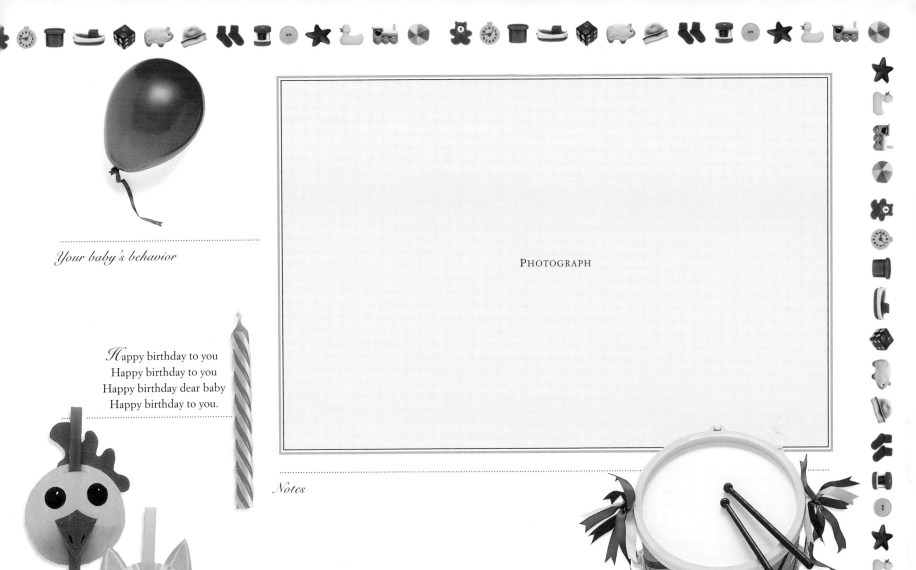

Your baby's behavior

*H*appy birthday to you
Happy birthday to you
Happy birthday dear baby
Happy birthday to you.

PHOTOGRAPH

Notes

Mankind owes to the child the best
it has to give.

United Nations Declaration

First smiles ....

First tooth ....

First discovers hands and feet ....

First crawls ....

First grasps object ....

First stands ....

First holds head up ....

First steps ....

First sits up ....

First waves goodbye ....

First kiss ....

First words ....

First haircut ....

First says Mama ....

First solid food ....

First says Dada ....

We find delight in the beauty and happiness of children that makes the heart too big for the body.

Ralph Waldo Emerson

First recognizes:

Mother

Father

Grandparents

Special friends

Animals

First friends

PHOTOGRAPH

Notes

MEMENTOS

Identification tag from hospital

Footprints

Handprints

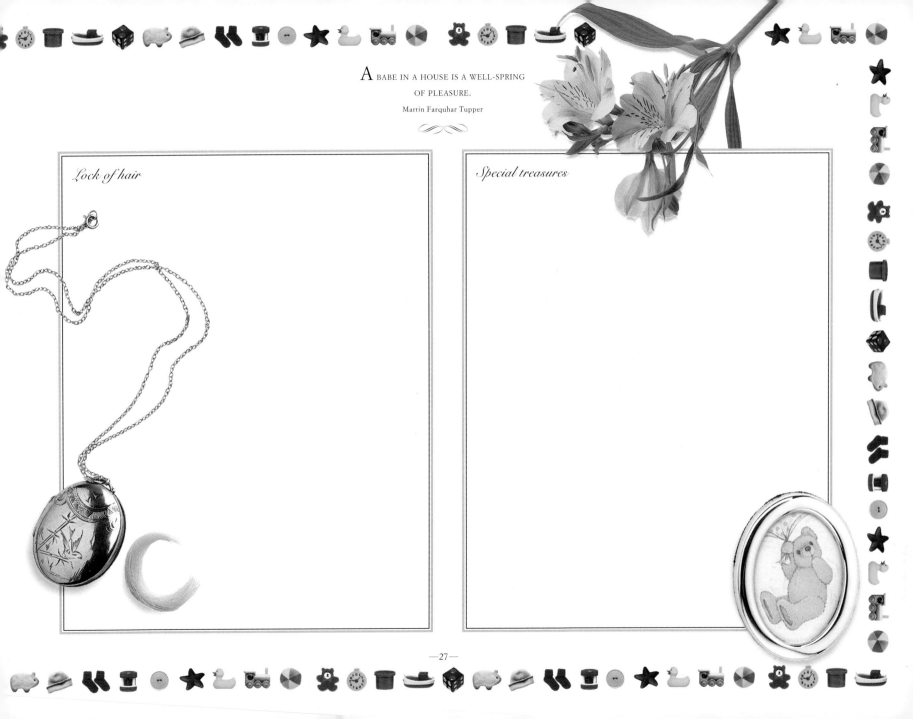

A BABE IN A HOUSE IS A WELL-SPRING
OF PLEASURE.

Martin Farquhar Tupper

Lock of hair

Special treasures

MEDICAL RECORD

THERE IS NO FINER INVESTMENT FOR ANY COMMUNITY THAN
PUTTING MILK INTO BABIES.

Winston Churchill

Immunization details

Vaccine	Age	Date
Diphtheria / Tetanus / Pertussis		
Polio		
Hemophilus b		
Measles / Mumps / Rubella		
Other		

Illnesses

Diagnosis	Age	Date

Visits to doctor

Reason   Age   Date

Allergies

Blood group

Eyesight test

Hearing test

AGE AND WEIGHT CHART

Weight   Age in months

lbs   kgs   0   1   2   3   4   5   6   7   8   9   10   11   12

Average for girls

Average for boys

Notes

SPECIAL MEMORIES

Of all the wonderful things to have happened during your baby's first year of life, some will stand out as particularly memorable and worth recording.

GIVE A LITTLE LOVE TO A CHILD, AND YOU
GET A GREAT DEAL BACK.

John Ruskin

HOPES FOR THE FUTURE

....

Plans for the future

....

Possible schools

....

Prediction of future occupation

....

Your baby's character

PERHAPS A CHILD WHO IS FUSSED OVER GETS A FEELING
OF DESTINY, HE THINKS HE IS IN THE WORLD FOR SOMETHING
IMPORTANT AND IT GIVES HIM DRIVE AND CONFIDENCE.

Benjamin Spock

PHOTOGRAPH

FROM .... TO ....

DAY 1	DAY 2	DAY 3	DAY 4		DAY 5	DAY 6
Date...........................						
DAY 7	DAY 8	DAY 9	DAY 10	DAY 11	DAY 12	DAY 13
DAY 14	DAY 15	DAY 16	DAY 17	DAY 18	DAY 19	DAY 20
	DAY 21	DAY 22	DAY 23	DAY 24	DAY 25	DAY 26
	DAY 27	DAY 28	DAY 29	DAY 30	DAY 31

Don't forget – start using the stickers to record your baby's development

FROM .... TO ....

Weight ....

Length ....

Sleeping pattern ....

....

Bedtime ....

Feeding pattern ....

....

Physical changes ....

....

Medical checkups ....

....

New sounds ....

PHOTOGRAPH

....

Date of photograph ....

Response to mother ....

A typical day ....

....

Response to father ....

....

FROM .... TO ....

PHOTOGRAPH

Weight ....

Length ....

Sleeping pattern ....

Bedtime ....

Feeding pattern ....

Physical changes ....

Medical checkups ....

New sounds ....

Date of photograph ....

A typical day

Response to mother ....

Response to father ....

FROM .... TO ....

DAY 1	DAY 2	DAY 3	DAY 4	DAY 5	DAY 6	DAY 7
Date						
DAY 8	DAY 9	DAY 10	DAY 11	DAY 12	DAY 13	DAY 14
DAY 15	DAY 16	DAY 17		DAY 18	DAY 19	DAY 20
DAY 21	DAY 22	DAY 23	DAY 24	DAY 25	DAY 26	
DAY 27	DAY 28	DAY 29	DAY 30	DAY 31		

MONTH 3

FROM .... TO ....

DAY 1	DAY 2	DAY 3	DAY 4	DAY 5	DAY 6	DAY 7
Date..........						
DAY 8	DAY 9		DAY 10	DAY 11	DAY 12	DAY 13
DAY 14	DAY 15	DAY 16	DAY 17	DAY 18	DAY 19	DAY 20
	DAY 21	DAY 22	DAY 23	DAY 24	DAY 25	DAY 26
	DAY 27	DAY 28	DAY 29	DAY 30	DAY 31	

FROM .... TO ....

Weight .... Length ....

Sleeping pattern ....

....

Wakes up ....

Bedtime ....

Feeding pattern ....

Medical checkups ....

Physical changes ....

....

New sounds ....

....

Response to mother ....

Response to father ....

A typical day ....

....

PHOTOGRAPH

Date of photograph

FROM   TO

Weight   Length

Sleeping pattern

Wakes up

Bedtime

Description of mealtime

Physical changes

New movements

New sounds

Medical checkups

Favorite activities

A typical day

PHOTOGRAPH

Date of photograph

FROM   TO

DAY
1

Date ....

DAY
2

DAY
3

DAY
4

DAY
5

DAY
6

DAY
7

DAY
8

DAY
9

DAY
10

DAY
11

DAY
12

DAY
13

DAY
14

DAY
15

DAY
16

DAY
17

DAY
18

DAY
19

DAY
20

DAY
21

DAY
22

DAY
23

DAY
24

DAY
25

DAY
26

DAY
27

DAY
28

DAY
29

DAY
30

DAY
31

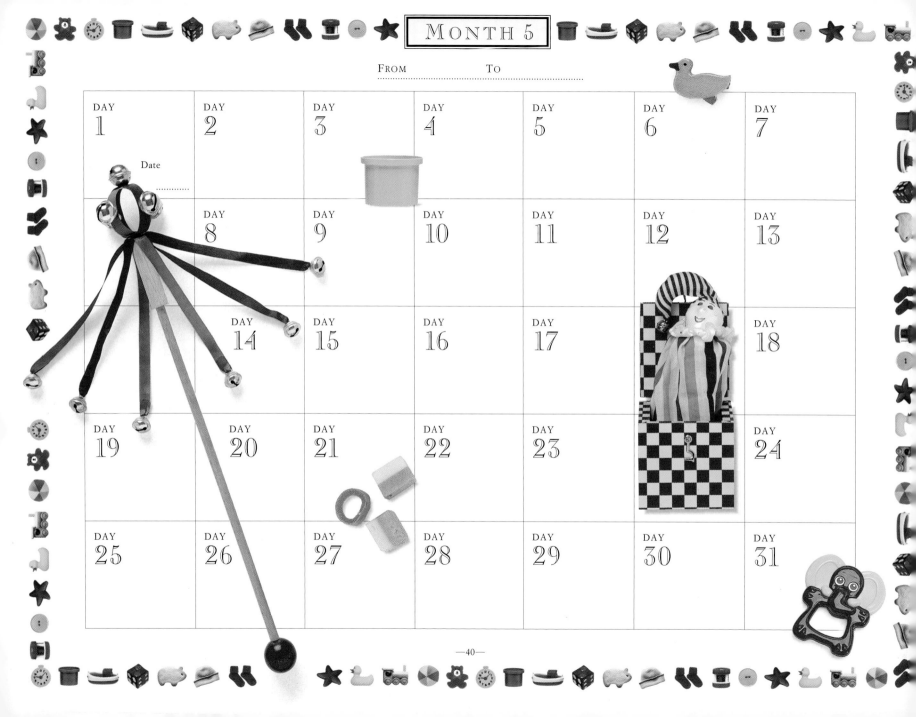

FROM …………………… TO ……………………

DAY 1	DAY 2	DAY 3	DAY 4	DAY 5	DAY 6	DAY 7
DAY — Date ………	DAY 8	DAY 9	DAY 10	DAY 11	DAY 12	DAY 13
	DAY 14	DAY 15	DAY 16	DAY 17		DAY 18
DAY 19	DAY 20	DAY 21	DAY 22	DAY 23		DAY 24
DAY 25	DAY 26	DAY 27	DAY 28	DAY 29	DAY 30	DAY 31

FROM _____ TO _____

Weight ....

Length ....

Sleeping pattern ....

....

Wakes up ....

Bedtime ....

Description of mealtime ....

....

Favorite foods ....

....

Medical checkups ....

PHOTOGRAPH

....

New movements ....

Physical changes ....

New sounds ....

Favorite activities ....

Date of photograph ....

Favorite outing ....

A typical day ....

FROM   TO

PHOTOGRAPH

Weight

Length

Sleeping pattern

Wakes up

Bedtime

Description of mealtime

Favorite foods

Medical checkups

Date of photograph

Favorite outing

A typical day

New movements

Physical changes

New sounds

Favorite activities

MONTH 6

FROM .... TO ....

DAY 1	DAY 2	DAY 3	DAY 4	DAY 5	DAY 6
Date					
DAY 7	DAY 8	DAY 9	DAY 10	DAY 11	DAY 12	DAY 13
DAY 14	DAY 15	DAY 16	DAY 17	DAY 18	DAY 19	DAY 20
DAY 21	DAY 22		DAY 23	DAY 24	DAY 25	
DAY 26	DAY 27	DAY 28	DAY 29	DAY 30	DAY 31	

FROM   TO
....

DAY 1	DAY 2	DAY 3	DAY 4	DAY 5	DAY 6	DAY 7
Date...........................	DAY 9	DAY 10			DAY 11	DAY 12
DAY 8						
DAY 13	DAY 14	DAY 15	DAY 16	DAY 17	DAY 18	DAY 19
	DAY 21	DAY 22	DAY 23	DAY 24	DAY 25	
DAY 20						
DAY 26	DAY 27	DAY 28	DAY 29	DAY 30	DAY 31	

FROM   TO

Weight

Length

Sleeping pattern

Wakes up

Bedtime

Description of mealtime

Favorite foods

PHOTOGRAPH

Medical checkups

Date of photograph

New movements

Favorite outing

Physical changes

A typical day

New sounds

Favorite activities

—45—

FROM .... TO ....

PHOTOGRAPH

Weight
....

Length
....

Sleeping pattern
....

Wakes up
....

Bedtime
....

Description of mealtime
....
....

Favorite foods
....
....

Medical checkups
....

Date of photograph
....

Favorite outing
....

A typical day
....

New movements
....

Physical changes
....

New sounds
....

Favorite activities
....

FROM .... TO ....

DAY 1	DAY 2	DAY 3	DAY 4	DAY 5	DAY 6	DAY 7
Date						
DAY 8	DAY 9	DAY 10	DAY 11	DAY 12	DAY 13	DAY 14
DAY 15		DAY 16	DAY 17	DAY 18	DAY 19	DAY 20
DAY 21		DAY 22	DAY 23	DAY 24	DAY 25	DAY 26
DAY 27	DAY 28	DAY 29	DAY 30	DAY 31		

FROM _____ TO _____

DAY
1

Date...................

DAY
2

DAY
3

DAY
4

DAY
5

DAY
6

DAY
7

DAY
8

DAY
9

DAY
10

DAY
11

DAY
12

DAY
13

DAY
14

DAY
15

DAY
16

DAY
17

DAY
18

DAY
19

DAY
20

DAY
21

DAY
22

DAY
23

DAY
24

DAY
25

DAY
26

DAY
27

DAY
28

DAY
29

DAY
30

DAY
31

MONTH 9

FROM .... TO ....

Weight .... Length ....

Sleeping pattern ....

Rises at ....

Bedtime ....

Description of mealtime ....

....

Physical changes ....

....

New movements ....

....

New sounds ....

....

Medical checks ....

Favorite activities ....

....

A typical day ....

....

PHOTOGRAPH

Date of photograph ....

FROM .... TO ....

Weight .... Length ....

Sleeping pattern ....

....

Wakes up ....

Bedtime ....

Description of mealtime ....

....

Physical changes ....

....

New movements ....

....

New sounds ....

....

Medical checkups ....

Favorite activities ....

....

A typical day ....

....

PHOTOGRAPH

Date of photograph

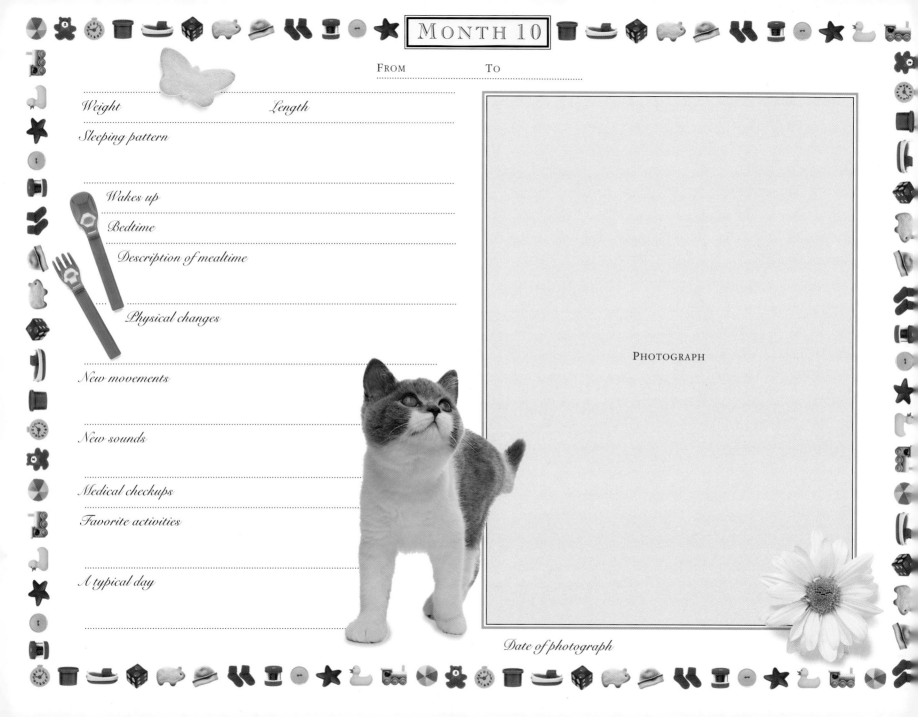

FROM .... TO ....

DAY 1	DAY 2	DAY 3	DAY 4	DAY 5	DAY 6	DAY 7
Date						
DAY 8	DAY 9	DAY 10	DAY 11	DAY 12	DAY 13	DAY 14
DAY 15		DAY 16	DAY 17	DAY 18	DAY 19	
DAY 20	DAY 21	DAY 22	DAY 23	DAY 24	DAY 25	
DAY 26	DAY 27	DAY 28	DAY 29	DAY 30	DAY 31	

FROM   TO

DAY 1

Date............................

DAY 2

DAY 3

DAY 4

DAY 5

DAY 6

DAY 7

DAY 8

DAY 9

DAY 10

DAY 11

DAY 12

DAY 13

DAY 14

DAY 15

DAY 16

DAY 17

DAY 18

DAY 19

DAY 20

DAY 21

DAY 22

DAY 23

DAY 24

DAY 25

DAY 26

DAY 27

DAY 28

DAY 29

DAY 30

DAY 31

FROM .... TO ....

Weight ....

Length ....

Sleeping pattern ....

....

Rises at ....

Bedtime ....

Description of mealtime ....

Favorite foods ....

....

Medical checks ....

New movements ....

Physical changes ....

New sounds ....

Favorite activities ....

PHOTOGRAPH

Date of photograph ....

Favorite outing ....

A typical day ....

FROM   TO

PHOTOGRAPH

Weight

Length

Sleeping pattern

Wakes up

Bedtime

Description of mealtime

Favorite foods

Medical checkups

Date of photograph

Favorite outing

A typical day

New movements

Physical changes

New sounds

Favorite activities

MONTH 12

FROM .... TO ....

	DAY 1 Date	DAY 2	DAY 3	DAY 4	DAY 5	DAY 6
DAY 7	DAY 8	DAY 9	DAY 10	DAY 11	DAY 12	DAY 13
DAY 14	DAY 15		DAY 16	DAY 17	DAY 18	DAY 19
DAY 20	DAY 21	DAY 22	DAY 23	DAY 24		DAY 25
DAY 26	DAY 27	DAY 28	DAY 29	DAY 30		DAY 31

A Dorling Kindersley book

Design Bernard Higton
Text Caroline Ash

First American Edition, 1995

2 4 6 8 10 9 7 5 3

Published in the United States by
Dorling Kindersley Publishing, Inc.,
95 Madison Avenue, New York, New York 10016

Visit us on the World Wide Web at
http://www.dk.com

Published in Great Britain by Dorling Kindersley Limited.
Distributed by Houghton Mifflin Company, Boston.

ISBN 1-56458-851-3
Color reproduction by Colorscan, Singapore
Printed and bound in China by Imago

Photography Stephen Oliver, Guy Ryecart,
Colin Keates Natural History Museum,
D K Studio